Poetry from

25 Years of

Southern Cultures

EVERLASTING

GABRIELLE CALVOCORESSI *&* MARINA GREENFELD,
EDITORS

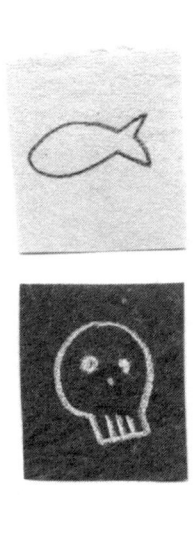

Table of Contents

Introduction

"BOUNTY EVERLASTING" seems a perfect way to describe poetry from twenty-five years of *Southern Cultures*. From its earliest days, the journal has featured poets whose ability to encapsulate and transform human experience is both quintessentially southern and a testament to their ability to make the most wide-ranging subjects feel deeply familiar and local to the reader. As we contemplated our poetic history, it was profoundly moving to see some of the most widely lauded and loved poets in the United States sitting in company with each other. Remarkable to see "Elegy for the Native Guards" by former Poet Laureate Natasha Trethewey in the same journal as Tiana Clark's "The Rime of Nina Simone" and Tom Andrews's "Praying with George Herbert In Late Winter."

Southern Cultures has always featured great poems from poets who are (or are destined to become) essential parts of the literary landscape. At the same time, there's an intimacy created within our pages. We feature four poets every year, so the accumulation of poems feels more like a conversation than a clamor of voices. And yet, the range of poetics and experiences speaks to the journal's deep understanding that poetry, like the South itself, is constantly evolving and opening outward even as it looks back to the hardest and most painful stories and utterances.

We hope you find some poems by poets you love and some by poets you haven't met yet. And we hope you'll celebrate with us as *Southern Cultures* continues to seek out and feature the vital voices in poetry, bringing news of the personal, the political, the painful, and the joyful. We're grateful to the poets and to you.

Bountifully,

Gabrielle Calvocoressi   Marina Greenfeld
Poetry Editor, *Southern Cultures*   Chapbook Editor, *Southern Cultures*

A List of Waters

TYREE DAYE

1.

The scar that flows from my aunt's thigh
to the boulder of her swollen ankle is a map
of the Haw River,
each toe a Blue Heron.

2.

My mama's water
        is all water, I'm every river rock
inside her being smoothed over.

3.

The palms of my uncle's hands
are the Deep River when he is holding a gutted trout.
Always something
is bleeding.

4.

You saw her bloody
and did nothing,
you Yellow Perch.

5.
My uncles sinned openly
on Sunday,
fed in the daytime,

    a White Catfish.

6.
My smallest cousin is a salamander in their father's

    Neuse River arms, legs hanging there
like Blackwater.

7.
Every woman
who has ever told me to clean my face
is the Atlantic Ocean.

8.
The shoreline of this beach
is also a history lesson,
these sea shells
have blood on them.

9.
I dream mostly in floods.

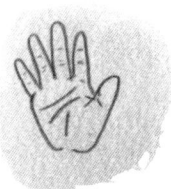 

Ethel's Sestina

PATRICIA SMITH

Ethel Freeman's body sat for days in her wheelchair outside the New Orleans Convention Center. Her son Herbert, who had assured his mother that help was on the way, was forced to leave her there once she died.

Gon' be obedient in this here chair,
gon' bide my time, fanning against this sun.
I ask my boy, and all he says is *Wait.*
He wipes my brow with steam, says I should sleep.
I trust his every word. Herbert my son.
I believe him when he says help gon' come.

Been so long since all these suffrin' folks come
to this place. Now on the ground 'round my chair,
they sweat in my shade, keep asking my son
could that be a bus they see. It's the sun
foolin' them, shining much too loud for sleep,
making us hear engines, wheels. Not yet. Wait.

Lawd, some folks prayin' for rain while they wait,
forgetting what rain can do. When it come,
it smashes living flat, wakes you from sleep,
eats streets, washes you clean out of the chair
you be sittin' in. Best to praise this sun,
shinin' its dry shine. *Lawd have mercy, son,*

is it coming? Such a strong man, my son.
Can't help but believe when he tells us, *Wait*.
Wait some more. Wish some trees would block this sun.
We wait. Ain't no white men or buses come,
but look — see that there? Get me out this chair,
help me stand on up. No time for sleepin',

Cause look what's rumbling this way. If you sleep
you gon' miss it. *Look there*, I tell my son.
He don't hear it. I'm 'bout to get out this chair,
but the ghost in my legs tells me to wait,
wait for the salvation that's sho to come.
I see my savior's face 'longside that sun.

Nobody sees me running toward the sun.
Lawd, they think I done gone and fell asleep.
They don't hear *Come*.

Come.
Come.
Come.
Come.
Come.
Come.
Ain't but one power make me leave my son.
I can't wait, Herbert. Lawd knows I can't wait.
Don't cry, boy, I ain't in that chair no more.

Wish you coulda come on this journey, son,
see that ol' sweet sun lift me out of sleep.
Didn't have to wait. And see my golden chair?

Semantic Relations

ADRIAN BLEVINS

Though naturally I love them they are a monstrosity, acute and unruly,
already pig-headed on the way from the airport to come and infect me

with what kind of mayonnaise is better than Hellmann's and which of us
got the new bike versus who crashed the old and who's drinking too much

versus who ought to get the special Weight-Watchers brownies
and who isn't on that plan but really should be and whose kid is in what university

versus whose kid is in which other. Yes I love them but they talk
    too much about nothing
because they are after pulling me out of the stillness I came up North for

because in their opinion I've always been too faraway
starting in the '70s like an anonymous planet up in my room

while they all sat around downstairs vehement on the topic
of everything I was missing because after all it was just the *hearth*—

just the kids pouring juice and telling jokes while the scant one upstairs
plotted some wraithlike escape like could she become some kind of particle?

 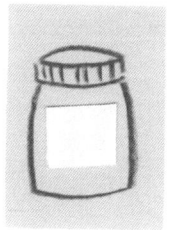 

Could she float out to sea maybe on a raft of splintered pillars?
This is part of the story of my people who won't say much

but rigorously chatter about global warming and formaldehyde and cancer
and Hemingway and Peter Jennings and Bush who we despise

because he is a killer. My people are not killers — they are romantics —
they like to sit around on porches and tell false stories

because lies are more agreeable than me eyeing them haughtily and saying
as a matter of fact, though I'm forced to do it because we're almost out

of time, O my high-hilled, prattling sweethearts — O my brothers and sisters
of hoodwink and swindle and fiddle and twaddle and drivel and hokum and tripe.

Autumn's Sidereal, November's a Ball and Chain

CHARLES WRIGHT

After the leaves have fallen, the sky turns blue again,
Blue as a new translation of Longinus on the sublime.
We wink and work back from its edges.
                              We walk around
Under its sequence of metaphors,
Looking immaculately up for the overlooked.
Or looking not so immaculately down for the same thing.

If there's nothing going on, there's no reason to make it up.
Back here, for instance, next to the cankered limbs of the plum
        trees,
We take a load off.
                      Hard frost on the grass blades and wild onion,
Invisibly intricate, so clear.
Pine needles in herringbone, dead lemon leaves, dead dirt.
The metaphysical world is meaningless today,

South wind retelling its autobiography
                           endlessly
Through the white pines, somesuch and susurration, shhh, shhh . . .

Call

ATSURO RILEY

It starts with the lamp that lamped our night our dirt.

Cause of this (wear-balded) red-mud ring going glow.

The old ever-voice (with the tear through it) intonating, rivering.

Souls and appetites (from holler, brink, and gully) lured and drawn.

The story-man encircling us binding us by lard-torch and ditty.

So.

In the beginning.

And it came to pass.

Wait'll I tell you.

Tale-flicker from his crackling throat; blackening (kerosened) cattail held high:

— *Some say what she'd gripped right then wadn't vine but bullsnake.*

— *Hadn't they clung tooth and claw to branch and bark.*

— *When the creekbend child got beat got hided fresh his mama broke her switch.*

— *Damned if dog-daisies beanstalks didn't fank up in the spokes.*

Our pulse.

Our (crescendo-timbrous) amphi-glade of bug-chirk, burgeon.

Well was it green as this ever.

Bright breath of the lamp that lamps our night.

(Our dirt).

My Aunt Smokes Another Lucky

MICHAEL MCFEE

She slips it out of its leatherette case,
an immaculate cartridge
she clenches between the red bow of her lips
while flicking her butane lighter,
sucking deeply until the tip
starts to crackle and glow like a fuse.

She snaps the lighter shut and blows smoke
through pursed lips over her shoulder,
lifting the Lucky between two rednail fingers
like somebody about to take an oath,
her hand's glamorous gesture
echoing the pale curve of her cheek.

She smokes her way through another story,
punctuates it with the Lucky
she keeps sharp with crisp drags and raps
into the Everglades souvenir ashtray.
She squints at her cigarette:
one bitter puff and she wrings its neck

in the overflowing nest of ashes,
the lipstick on its butt so alluring
that when I start smoking candy cigarettes
I put the lit end in my mouth
and everybody laughs, especially my aunt,
smoke haunting her head like ghosts of family.

Is for, to Hold

BOB HICOK

I didn't tell the water it was a pitchfork.
I believe the water believed it was a trident
on account of the family resemblance.
The road had disappeared, the field,
the sundial was about to go under, meaning shadows
would have been unable to stay on schedule.
When I touched the water with the pitchfork,
it stopped rising, and for a week, an ocean
lived in the valley. Birds landed on the ocean
like this is what an ocean is for, to hold.
A few trees went by and a For Sale sign,
I called the number, how much to buy
this ocean? The pitchfork
had only turned over leaves and banana peels
into compost. I let it sit with us
at the table, fed it bratwurst and jaw breakers.
During the last flood, someone died
down the way, someone is always dying
when living is called for. We are not fish,
goes the saying, anymore. My neighbor
who lost his house, says it'll be awhile
before he can stare a glass of water in the face.
We are mostly water, mostly rain, people drown
in themselves. The ocean's a river again
and back where it sleeps. In the middle,
a refrigerator's a new island
of cool & white. I wade into the music of caress
and open the door, let water out into the water,
it swims away, everything swims away,
as the river nudges me, follow.

Elegy for the Native Guards

NATASHA TRETHEWEY

> *Now that the salt of their blood*
> *Stiffens the saltier oblivion of the sea . . .*
> *—Allen Tate*

We leave Gulfport at noon; gulls overhead
trailing the boat—streamers, noisy fanfare—
all the way to Ship Island. What we see
first is the fort, its roof of grass, a lee—
half reminder of the men who served there—
a weathered monument to some of the dead.

Inside we follow the ranger, hurried
though we are to get to the beach. He tells
of graves lost in the Gulf, the island split
in half when Hurricane Camille hit,
shows us casemates, cannons, the store that sells
souvenirs, tokens of history long buried.

The Daughters of the Confederacy
has placed a plaque here, at the fort's entrance—
each Confederate soldier's name raised hard
in bronze; no names carved for the Native Guards—
2nd Regiment, Union men, black phalanx.
What is monument to their legacy?

All the grave markers, all the crude headstones—
water-lost. Now fish dart among their bones,
and we listen for what the waves intone.
Only the fort remains, near forty feet high,
round, unfinished, half open to the sky,
the elements—wind, rain—God's deliberate eye.

Praying with George Herbert in Late Winter

TOM ANDREWS

I

In fits and starts, Lord,
  our words work
the other side of language

where you lie if you can be said
  to lie. Mercy upon
the priest who calls on you

to nurture and to terrorize
  him, for you oblige.
Mercy upon you, breath's engine

returning what is to what is.
  Outside, light swarms
and particularizes the snow;

tree limbs crack with ice
  and drop. I can say
there is a larger something

inside me. I can say,
  "Gratitude is
a strange country." But what

would I give to live there?

2

Something breaks in us,
and keeps breaking. Charity,
   be severe with me.
Mercy, lay on your hands.

   White robes on
the cypress tree. Sparrows
   clot the fence posts;
they hop once and weave

   through the bleached air.
Lord, I drift on the words
   I speak to you—
the words take on

   and utter me. In what
language are you not
   what *we* say you are?
Surprise me, Lord, as a seed

   surprises itself . . .

3

Today the sun has the inward look
of the eye of the Christ child.
   Grace falls at odd angles from heaven

   to earth: my sins are bright sparks
in the dark of blamelessness . . .
   Yes. From my window I watch a boy step

   backwards down the snow-covered road,
studying his sudden boot tracks.
   The wedding of his look and the world!

   And for a moment, Lord, I think
I understand about you and silence . . .
   But what a racket I make in telling you.

Crowd Crush

EMILIA PHILLIPS

I need to start being honest
with my constituents — the mirror

and hemlock, the just barely parted
blinds and, behind them,

my naked body in its easy labors
of making

coffee and sighing heavily.
I dare someone to accidentally

glimpse my nude
pantomime of minding my own

business. Sometimes I've got to be angry to be in
the mood for being

angry. Some people would release
a sex tape

before their taxes. How do I
account for the bottom line

of my booty I have to look over
my shoulder to see

in the mirror? Or the clutch in my gut every
time I see his hands, strong

in their aching, flex absentmindedly when
he

writes something down? Every time I see
her bottom lip so swollen

that her lipstick prints upside-
down on her chin,

I want to take impressions
of the *Times* with silly putty,

the news suddenly
RAW [   ] STUC

[   ] MSIRORRET ,
a truth I'd stretch—

if I could get away
with it without laughing.

Threads, End of Another Day

MICHAEL CHITWOOD

Threads would cling to them,
pants, purses, yokes of dresses,
as they walked or trotted
across the parking lot, released
by the four o'clock bell.

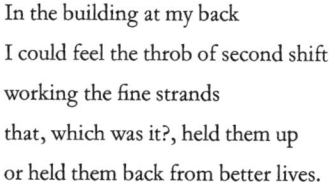

In the building at my back
I could feel the throb of second shift
working the fine strands
that, which was it?, held them up
or held them back from better lives.

Country tunes trailed them out the gate
while I waited for my ride, my evening.
The chainlink trolled those still moments
with its shadow net, and sparrows
gathered the string they let go.

That's it, all that happened, then, there,
and again, here, now, clinging to another day
where I'm working them in.
What you notice becomes your life.

first meeting

DÉLANA R. A. DAMERON

Some women suffer themselves fools
trying to hold a man

who floats between them like driftwood;
whose happy tongue slicks

his catfish back; who constricts
his lover's bones

as if a black rat snake
while holding out magnolia

blossom & eucalyptus branch offerings — except

for Annie who is strong as a water oak;
evergreen as pine.

Goldsboro narrative #11

FORREST HAMER

I sorely do love her, I thought he said.
Actually, he said he loved her surely,
but Southerners mix words up sometimes
and I have often taken them at face value.

So as this Southern man was talking about
the Southern woman he would marry,

it seemed to me grownups tangled their feelings
unnecessarily, and especially love. And,
since we were in Goldsboro and it was 1969,
I thought the confusion had to do with race—

with whether integration would work, even
if we called it desegregation (he didn't

believe it would). Or maybe she didn't love him at all
but was afraid to die by herself and
he was as good as the men who wouldn't come along:
surely this could work. That word again.

On the face of it, we know things and we know
even that we don't. We don't seem to do well with

the rest—whatever it is that trips
chaos into *talk-and-listen*, makes us mix up things.
Or, if race doesn't really explain, then
how do we explain these feelings we have about race?

I was asking the man how he thought our town would do
sending different children to the same schools.

He was in love, he protested, and he just wanted
the South to stay as it was for now,
not get into tangling things.

Legend

AL MAGINNES

Because I know her name from
rock and roll biographies
and the legendary death
of her first husband, because
I grew up hearing her voice
on my father's folk records,
because I love the myths
that accompany music
almost as much as I love
music, I should have gone
to see her when she was booked
into the coffeehouse run
by a church whose articles
of faith have been held secret
from all but the devout,
because better than teachers
and classmates I remember
those times a line from a song
chilled or awakened me from
the seemingly endless sleep
that is childhood, and she,
as much as any, could claim
some of those moments. But
I did not want to hear her if
it meant I would have to be
proselytized by shiny-
faced acolytes of the brand
of salvation peddled there
with coffee and cookies,
and why would she be singing
in such a place if she was not
a walker on that secret path.

Still, my whole family sang
her songs, those quick instances
of harmony rising from
the record's dusty grooves
to claim a place in the myth
of my family as well
as in the rock and roll myths
I once memorized
the way others learn scripture.
Like most who went to hear her,
I would have only been there
to gaze briefly on the altar
of her past, not to hear her
new songs or her new faith
Faith is what we have left
once we survive, even though
we owe our past the kindness
of a visit now and then.
Time might have
warmed and deepened her voice
that could once reach high enough
to freeze bone at its marrow,
but I didn't go and now
whenever I read or hear
her name I'll know she was
right down the street, singing songs
I don't remember not knowing,
Even if all she had done
was chant the famous names
of her dead husband or her
new god, even if she denied
completely or insisted
upon being defined by
her past, even if time has
done to her what it has done
to all of us, I should have gone.

American Honey

JOY PRIEST

It's easier than you thought—leaving.
Only one night spent sleeping on your own
in a motel parking lot beneath the stars
of a summer Muskogee. Your long-built dread
dispersing like gas into a brilliantly black
Ozark sky. For once, you are a girl

unmolested. You could do this: be a girl
without a home. Always gone. Perpetually leaving
behind Strip Mall, U.S.A & the dark
green dumpster you raid for food, something to own
& the two kids no one will take care of & the dread
that comes on when their father squeezes your ass. Star,

let your freedom build slow like the death of a star
across the years. & when she calls for you—granddaughter
of Elvis, confederate flag bikini, voice you dread—
let the interstate's roar swallow her sound. In your leaving
you see the country for the first time. Your very own
seeing. When he howls for you, your body is a silent, black

barn hidden in wild grass & your locs—pastoral, black—
are ropes for him, swinging from its rafters. Death star.
It's easier than you imagined—leaving behind your own
mother. Her ghost. Her meth. And now you can be a girl
on a back patio with three white men, & you can leave
with their money, egg suede cowboy hat adorning your dreads.

You swallowed the Mezcal worm of your fear.
Now you're standing in the cowboy's convertible, black
& flying in the camera's frame. You're leaving
with the get-away boy you found sparkling
in a K-mart parking lot. You're keeping it alive—your girlhood,
the adrenaline, the novelty, the dying star that you own

a million miles away. You're learning how to own
yourself, how to be 14-deep in a 12-seater without dread,
how to be disarmed, how to let it go when the white girl
from Florida says nigga again, how to be the only black
girl among strangers, dancing around a bonfire under the stars,
singing out of the sunroof down the interstate. Leaving

each new town you meet and own a memory in, leaving
behind your mother's dread-veined eye. Her tragic star.
Learn it all, girl, until what you've left behind is a brilliant black.

From "The Rime of Nina Simone"

TIANA CLARK

Argument

*How a Slave Ship was driven by capitalism and racism inside the triangle
of the transatlantic slave trade; and of the strange things that befell;
and in what manner Nina Simone came back from the dead to her
own Country to stop a graduate student on the way to workshop.*

. . .

I didn't recognize her at first,
but felt urgency inside her glittering
eyes—grotesque and morganite,
melting blooms. Her skin, stabbed

with hammered copper, afro nimbus,
the luminous gaze, an X-ray swishing
at my skin with metronomic waves.
Timeworn but regal, her spine

made of satin and salt, her bolted
black back clutching every battle-born
ballad: a lone column of glissandos
and thunder snow, booming and bright.

Come here, she says.

Sorry, I can't—I'm late. I'm—

I need to tell you something   about yourself.

Listen, little girl:

For every pain
there is a longer   song.

                    The body pours

                                        its own music.

                          I wanted
                          to play Bach
                          and Beethoven
                          for endless encores. But

they wouldn't let me
and they won't let you.

                    . . .

The art of tamping — espresso — folding dark meadows inside
              my throat: fluttering uvula, lone pink hibiscus in praise.

                                        I unbuckled my trauma
                                        one note at a time.

                    One note at a time

                                        I un-buck-led
                                        my trauma.

          Woke up
          drenched in cold sweat
          and furiously
          tried to remember
          my only dream:

                                        FINALLY

          playing a Bach
          cantata at Carnegie Hall

                                        FINALLY

the audience would
shut up and listen

in the way
I needed them to listen   to me.

All   quiet
as fresh snow muffling
early morning trees,
a hushing frost
on the meadow sparkling
with untracked fondant.

But it never happened. They only
wanted cocktail jazz, folk, and blues,

for me to bleed negro, a signifyin(g)
monkey from my classical piano.

They only wanted that *Swing low*,
Sweet chariot strain, but I smashed it all

together anyway, making and breaking
forms on the bridge between my voice

and finger play. My vinyl sorrow spinning,
spinning the grind against cuspate needle.

My records swarthy as the beloved skin
of Cain, bitten. I silenced the audience

with one   long   glare.

She pauses to show me her famous Midtown stare.

Like a ghost ship, I wandered from stages to states
and countries and colleges, concert after concert.

> I unglued
> > myself
> > in hotel mirrors
> > until I disappeared
> > visions of laser beams
> > and skin, always skin
> > sliced with heaven,
> > lingering scent
> > of a burnt-out
> > bulb — still,
> > incandescent,
> > the weirdness.

> They said my blue note
> baritone could find the tiniest sack
> > of unsent tears   inside
> > anybody. Any   body.

> Called me Black Bitch: Diva. Demanding. Difficult.
> Depressed. Genius. Monster.

They don't call me that here. *Well, not to my face.*
I can write about anything I want. *I think.* Here…
here are the dead bodies and bullets in my work.
Here are the four little girls, I say as I hold up my poems.

> Look, if you can write about anything   you want,
> > Then write. About. Anything.   *You* want.
> > Why do you keep panting & hunting   black hurt,
> > black scars like a slave-breaker?   Why scratch
> > the white page, a master,   for old blood?
> > Like a god, you are   so thirsty,
> > hell-bent on carving beauty   from dead bodies
> > from sacrifice   on the altar.

Because

I listen to the trees
humming through the Poplar leaves

and Southern magnolias. Bloated faces,
these beauteous forms, still swinging,

limp pendulum, waxy bleach-white blooms,
egg whites inside hardboiled eyes

sway and rock, roll forward, fragrant.
I'm ready to find the ruined churches.

I have a second stomach now. Now
I can look at my dead   and listen.

Listen, I'm transcribing the soaked,
splattered leaves —

                    You sound so tired, my darling…
                                        You weary yet?
                    she whispers in my ear, of creating and fighting…
                    can you stay a dog chained
                    barking at every threat, out of breath
                    in the darkness — and the darkness
                    is always you — panting for more food
                    to get published, for what? This?

Yes. This:
I need to be here — in the workshop.
I must look them in the face
and tell them when their words
and worlds are making me uncomfortable.
Tell them my body is real — not imagined,

not a prop or sieve or a literary device.
I must tell them that I. Am. Here. You cannot
write around me. The periphery is also mine.
I'm not afraid to take up the space I need to survive.
I'm not afraid to write what I need to survive.

> Mmmmm...write what *you* need, ha!
> Be careful now. They might snatch that money back real quick
> > when you start talking revolutionary—
> > what's your compulsion?

The Slave Ship :: war machine.
Robert Hayden's *Jesus   Saviour   Pilot   Me.*

I can't talk about the trees
without the blood.

contributors

TOM ANDREWS (1961–2001) authored two critically acclaimed books of poetry, *The Brother's Country* and *The Hemophiliac's Motorcycle*. A recipient of the 1999 Prix de Rome Fellowship in Literature from the American Academy of Arts and Letters, his literary awards include an Academy of American Poets Prize and the Iowa Poetry Prize. In the words of his teacher Charles Wright: "Tom was singular and luminous, as is his work. All of us, each one of us, will leave a space, an emptiness, when we die. But all of us, when we go, will not, as Tom did, turn out a light."

ADRIAN BLEVINS is the author of the full-length poetry collections *Appalachians Run Amok*, *Live from the Homesick Jamboree*, *The Brass Girl Brouhaha*, the chapbooks *Bloodline* and *The Man Who Went Out for Cigarettes*, and a co-edited collection of essays, *Walk Till the Dogs Get Mean: Meditations on the Forbidden from Contemporary Appalachia*. She is the recipient of many awards and honors, including the Wilder Prize, the Kate Tufts Discovery Award, and a Rona Jaffe Writer's Foundation Award. She teaches at Colby College in Waterville, Maine.

MICHAEL CHITWOOD served as poetry editor of *Southern Cultures* for sixteen years. His most recent book, *Search & Rescue*, received the 2018 L. E. Phillabaum Prize from LSU Press.

TIANA CLARK is the author of the debut poetry collection *I Can't Talk About the Trees Without the Blood* (University of Pittsburgh Press, 2018), winner of the 2017 Agnes Lynch Starrett Prize, and *Equilibrium* (Bull City Press, 2016), selected by Afaa Michael Weaver for the 2016 Frost Place Chapbook Competition. Clark is a 2019 National Endowment for the Arts Literature Fellow and a recipient of a 2019 Pushcart Prize, as well as a winner of the 2017 Furious Flower's Gwendolyn Brooks Centennial Poetry Prize and 2015 Rattle Poetry Prize. She was the 2017–2018 Jay C.

and Ruth Halls Poetry Fellow at the Wisconsin Institute of Creative Writing. Her writing has appeared in or is forthcoming from the *New Yorker*, *Poetry*, *Callaloo*, *Kenyon Review*, *VQR*, *American Poetry Review*, *Best New Poets 2015*, and elsewhere.

DÉLANA R. A. DAMERON is the author of *Weary Kingdom* and *How God Ends Us*. She is an arts and culture strategist and divides her time between Columbia, South Carolina, and Brooklyn, New York.

TYREE DAYE is a poet from Youngsville, North Carolina. He is a recipient of a 2019 Whiting Award.

FORREST HAMER is a Goldsboro native, and the author of three poetry collections, *Call & Response* (Alice James), *Middle Ear* (Roundhouse), and *Rift* (Four Way Books).

BOB HICOK'S most recent book is *Hold* (Copper Canyon, 2018).

AL MAGINNES is the author of eleven collections of poetry. He lives in Raleigh, North Carolina, and teaches at Wake Technical Community College.

MICHAEL MCFEE, recipient of the 2018 North Carolina Award for Literature, has published eleven books of poetry, two collections of essays, and anthologies of contemporary N.C. poems and short stories.

EMILIA PHILLIPS is the author of three poetry collections, most recently *Empty Clip* (University of Akron Press, 2018). She is assistant professor of creative writing at the University of North Carolina at Greensboro.

JOY PRIEST grew up in Louisville, Kentucky, across the street from the world's most famous horseracing track. She is the recipient of the 2018 Gregory Pardlo Fellowship at The Frost Place, and has received support from the Hurston/Wright Foundation, the Bread Loaf Writers' Conference, and the Fine Arts Work Center at Provincetown. She is editor emerita at *Yemassee*, and her poems have appeared or are forthcoming in *Blackbird*, *Callaloo*, *Four Way Review*, *Gulf Coast*, *The Rumpus*, and *Best New Poets 2014* & *2016*.

ATSURO RILEY is the author of *Romey's Order*, winner of the Kate Tufts Discovery Award, the Whiting Award, the Believer Poetry Award, and the Witter Bynner Award from the Library of Congress. He lives in San Francisco.

PATRICIA SMITH is the author of eight books of poetry, including *Incendiary Art*, a finalist for the 2018 Pulitzer Prize.

NATASHA TRETHEWEY is the author of six poetry collections, including *Native Guard*, which won the 2007 Pulitzer Prize. She served as the U.S. Poet Laureate from 2012 to 2014, and is a Chancellor of the Academy of American Poets..

CHARLES WRIGHT lives in Charlottesville, Virginia. He has retired from teaching at the University of Virginia. His new book *Oblivion Banjo*, a selection from his collected works, is forthcoming spring 2019.

$outhern
CULTURES

EDITORS	Harry Watson and Marcie Cohen Ferris
EXECUTIVE EDITOR	Ayse Erginer
DEPUTY EDITOR & ART DIRECTOR	Emily Wallace
ASSOCIATE EDITOR	Emma Calabrese
POETRY EDITOR	Gabrielle Calvocoressi
MUSIC EDITOR	Aaron Smithers
MEDIA & PRODUCTION	Ashley Melzer
SCHOLARLY OUTREACH	Kathy Roberts
EDITORIAL FELLOW	Katharine Henry
EDITORIAL ASSISTANTS	Marina Greenfeld Mitra Norowzi
DESIGNER	Hudd Byard
ILLUSTRATOR	Amy S. Hoppe
FOUNDING EDITOR	John Shelton Reed

Center for the Study of the American South

Malinda Maynor Lowery, *Director*

Southern Cultures Copyright © 2019 Center for the Study of the
American South Indexed in Humanities International Complete.
Back issues are available through www.SouthernCultures.org.
All poems reprinted with permission.